YOUR KNOWLEDGE HAS VALUE

Bibliographic information published by the German National Library:

The German National Library lists this publication in the National Bibliography; detailed bibliographic data are available on the Internet at http://dnb.dnb.de .

Imprint:

Copyright © 2014 GRIN Verlag
Print and binding: Books on Demand GmbH, Norderstedt Germany
ISBN: 9783668740587

This book at GRIN:

https://www.grin.com/document/430852

Tom Fengel

The Blaxploitation Film and its Influence on the Image of African Americans

GRIN Verlag

GRIN - Your knowledge has value

Since its foundation in 1998, GRIN has specialized in publishing academic texts by students, college teachers and other academics as e-book and printed book. The website www.grin.com is an ideal platform for presenting term papers, final papers, scientific essays, dissertations and specialist books.

Visit us on the internet:

http://www.grin.com/

http://www.facebook.com/grincom

http://www.twitter.com/grin_com

Technische Universität Dresden
Fakultät Sprach-, Literatur- und Kulturwissenschaften
Institut für Anglistik und Amerikanistik
Wintersemester 2014/2015
Seminar: Multicultural America

Seminar Paper:
The Blaxploitation Film and its Influence on the Image of African Americans

Vorgelegt von:	Tom Fengel
Studiengang:	Höheres Lehramt für Gymnasien
Fächer:	Englisch – Philosophie
Semester:	1. Fachsemester (Master)
Datum:	21.03.2014

Table of Contents

1 Introduction

"Who is the black private dick that's a sex machine to all the chicks? [...]
Who is the man that would risk his neck for his brother man?" (Shaft)

The person Isaac Hayes is asking for in these introductory lyrics is Shaft from the same-titled movie. Already in these few lines, the audience can be sure of the film genre they are going to have a look at then – It is Blaxploitation!

Throughout the history of film, African Americans struggled to establish a realistic cinematic representation of themselves without stereotyping, exaggerated clichés or even the mere display of black suppression and humiliation. While some of these points can be argued about in the genre of Blaxploitation, at least the latter two should not be true in it. Here we see a black hero who seems to be as sovereign as no African American in literature or film did ever before.

In this paper, it is my objective to examine the characterization of black Americans in Blaxploitation movies to evaluate its influence on the image of African Americans. Not only the cinematic image is to be questioned in this concern, but also the real impression these movies gave to their viewers which also had an impact on the real life, social experience. Thereby, we can differentiate between the black image it produced for blacks, and the impression it left on the white spectators. For this purpose, I will firstly explain the phenomenon of Blaxploitation, its content and structure and name some examples. After that, the historical and social background of this genre is to be analyzed in order to explain how it could emerge and why it vanished as quickly as it came into existence. The depiction of African Americans in film before the 1970s is as important for further comprehension as is the rising political consciousness in the 1960s United States of America which found expression in the Civil Rights Movement.

After I have shown the background knowledge concerning Blaxploitation, the description of the image of black people depicted in these movies will follow by analyzing the film "Shaft" and collecting other significant characteristics of this illustration in the genre in general, using the literature on this topic. The analysis will be divided into a plot analysis and a film analysis, whereby the plot will show characteristics which are visible by a mere reflection of the storyline and setting. The film analysis afterwards will have to find said aspects in selected scenes from the movie itself. As the most appropriate books for the paper's intention, I chose "Framing Blackness" by Ed Guerrero and "Black and

White Media" by Karen Ross. Another interesting work, which suits as an informal guide to various Blaxploitation films, is the book "That's Blaxploitation!" by Darius James. Furthermore, the role and portrayal of women in these films is to be observed concerning the books by Ross and Guerrero and the analysis of "Shaft".

On this basis, I want to consider in the end whether the genre of Blaxploitation had a more positive or negative impact on the cinematic and real image of African Americans, whereas this conclusion will presumably not be a simple statement of good or bad. Moreover, it is to be seen whether and how it influenced the social life of American black citizens and the future cinematic illustration of African Americanism.

The relevancy of the examination and evaluation of the influence of this genre finds its source in the very different reception of these films among African American themselves. In the time of the boom of Blaxploitation, and of course until today, these movies had and have been controversial for all its audience.

2 What is Blaxploitation?

2.1 The Blaxploitation Formula

Blaxploitation is the term used to describe movies made roughly between 1969 and 1974 which were cheaply produced and followed the "exploitation" patterns with a black cast. The concept of exploitation includes the aim to produce a filmic work at low financial costs and achieve a disproportionate earning by setting it in a sensational topic and context. Hollywood supported the financial success of the Blaxploitation wave immensely because it meant a huge economic outcome (Ross 18). Its target group was mostly the inner-city black youth audience (Guerrero 69), which strongly reacted to the wave's impulse and the genre's crucial core: The "aggressive black hero who beats the system and ends up with the money and the woman." (Ross 18). This essential core could be formulated as a recipe which was transferred to a lot of other works and resulted in the anticipated financial success of the exploitation scheme. The so-called Blaxploitation formula appealed to the black audience in a high manner and so the cinemas filled with little effort. The formula itself is broken down by Guerrero most adequately:

"[The Blaxploitation formula] usually consists of a pimp, gangster, or their baleful female counterparts, violently acting out a revenge or retribution motif against corrupt whites in the romanticized confines of the ghetto or inner city." (94)

The protagonist does not obligatorily have to be a pimp or gangster living a foremost illegal life. At least he (or she) is always a tough guy or female who powerfully pursues his or her goals and is not afraid to use, at least, semi-legal methods. But nevertheless, the audience watches an image of what is perceived as personified ghetto life. So, apart from the 'blackness factor', these movies follow the simple, traditional violent-action-hero of Hollywood, like the James Bond series. But on the other side, it was the first real opportunity for African American filmmakers to portray their communities in full, bright colors, even when most often supervised by the white Hollywood production elite. Melvin Van Peebles, who created the first and ground-setting work of the genre – "Sweet Sweetbacks Baadasssss Song" (in the following: SSAS), articulated his intentions by saying that he wanted a "victorious film" which encouraged its black audience to leave the theaters proudly and giving the feeling that "they'd had it" (Guerrero 88). So the film should wake a proud black consciousness of identity with an illustration of black power and the celebration of African American community and inner-city life. On the other side

5

however, critics stated that the genre only used more subtle ways of stereotyping to exploit the display of superficial blackness for entertainment purposes (Ross 62, 63).

Another important feature of Blaxploitation is the excessive display on sexuality. The male hero's masculinity is not only expressed by his aggression, but also by his ability to please every woman he wants to. This is to be seen as the reaction to the long time of desexualization of African American in film which then compensated with exaggerated force.

2.2 The Blaxploitation Wave

As already mentioned, the first great success of this type of films, which as well started the popularity boom of it, was SSBS in 1971. It shows a black man brought up in a Los Angeles inner-city brothel entertaining people with live sex shows. One night he flees from the police, which suspects him falsely of murder on a black man, to present him as a scapegoat and release him afterwards. The protagonist then leads a montage of his escape from the police through the ghettoes of Los Angeles dealing with the 'typical' black life there, including drug-dealers, prostitutes and various kinds of criminal activities carried out by blacks. On his way he has to seduce but also rape black and white women, as well fight different racial gangs and the police. In the end, he escapes to Mexico and the movie fades out not without a notice of revenge. The movie surrogates a sovereign African American, who cherishes but also fights the constituents of his community life, enforces his own perception of right and wrong, and wins the battle against the suppressive, white establishment. Thus, many members of the black community felt empowered as well as a notion of hope for the success of African American revolt against the inequality of their real life, social America. SSBS was followed by a flood of imitations, which simply followed the set formula naming "Superfly" and "Shaft" as the most successful and significant. But also references to film or literacy classics had been transformed into the black setting so that Bram Stoker's "Dracula" became "Blacula" or further interpretations like "Black Jesus", "Black Caesar" or the "Black Godfather" were created. For the black heroine the most noticeable works are to mention "Cleopatra Jones" and "Foxy Brown" which will be elaborated on in section 4.4. One interpretation of this transfer on the classics could be that African Americans should get the feeling that their 'culture' mattered and could also apply to some of the world's big and culturally important works.

6

The demand for this cheaply produced form of black relevancy resulted in the production of 91 movies between 1970 and 1973 which can be classified as Blaxploitation of which 47 followed the rule of the Blaxploitation formula (Guerrero 95). Observing such a dimension of nearly 100 films in only three years for one genre, the term exploitation receives certain clarity.

3 Historical and Socio-Cultural Backgrounds

3.1 The African American Image in Film before 1970

Before and around the time of World War II, the depiction of African Americans in the American film was still characterized by old stereotypes. In the 1940 classic "Gone With the Wind", they are shown in the motif of the "faithful servant and happy black folks." (Ross 14). This portrayal of African Americans as the servant of a white person, but on the other hand side their peaceful and satisfied attitude was what Ross declares as a justification of years of slavery and the superiority of white people, while the suppressed blacks took no offence by that and left the white audience in a feeling of innocence (14). Besides, African American actors even had to be painted darker and adopt 'standard' black behavior to really illustrate the black stereotype that was commonly expected by a white audience in those days (Ross 14). While some actors refused to play such humiliating roles, others pragmatically took the chance of earning one hundred times the money of a job by acting it (Ross 15). Nevertheless, one could argue that the black image underwent an improvement in film since World War I, when African American lost a commonly used depiction as villain or dangerous, evil threat by compromising it with the ridiculous and foolish minstrel figure. Otherwise the part of the African American in a movie would be characterized as naïve and friendly Uncle Tom. Also to avoid sexual stereotyping, a lot of black roles got desexualized around mid-nineteenth century, so that a sensual black person in film would be clearly irritating (Guerrero 62).

After World War II, the significant black acting talent, Sidney Poitier, emerged as a main black character in many movies. Throughout the 1950s and 1960s, he played the African American as a more intelligent human than before, and the black image gained dignity, but also fell into a stereotype of the black saint who sacrifices himself for whites and blacks out of religious conviction. Ross describes this image as more graceful than before but still as quiet and powerless in contrast to his white fellowship for which he is willing to give his life. Hence, the African American image improved, but always stayed underneath the superiority of the white man (16). Cripps comes to the conclusion that, also in his leading roles, Poitier furthermore played white characters in black skin instead of an authentic African American (Ross 17). In the time of the Civil Rights Movement, African American then were portrayed in a more heroic fashion for pacification reasons, as Ross implies. These roles illustrated blacks as savior, but never really let them have institutional

8

power (17). A rising popularity of black ex-athletes beginning acting careers led to the image of the macho African American man who is depicted as manly and desirable, but still not sexual available and always under control of a white superior (Guerrero 78). There were also authentically characterized African Americans, as the screening of black-written literature promised financial success. However, Ross states that the depiction of blackness ended in a general ambiguity of victim and problem (18). On the one hand side, blacks had to be agreed to have been suppressed by long periods of inequality in the USA because of the then current pressure by the Civil Rights Movement. On the other side, a realistic presentation of African Americanism usually resulted in a pitiful but non-sympathetic image of impoverished and criminal black communities, which more had the notion of "looking upon" than "feeling with" them.

In conclusion, the image of the African American in film right before 1970 consisted of a desexualized, quiet, intelligent but powerless person. He or she is either lucky enough to experience the leadership of a white man, or suffers from the poor conditions in the black community.

3.2 The Civil Rights Movement and a New African American Attitude

In the 1960s, the Civil Rights Movement demanded racial equality and an empowerment of racial minorities. While most middle-class and intellectual African Americans fought for a peaceful and civilized move towards racial equality by a certain willingness of assimilation, if the opportunity would be given to them, other organized groups formed with the intention to violently realize their rights if necessary. The image of the quiet, black saint lost its function of appeasement as Watts states in "Framing Blackness" that the perceived majority of African American saw themselves as "opposite [...] of what Negroes said Negroes were" (qtd. in Guerrero 89). This means that while the intellectual leaders of the equality movement propagated the black identity of a peaceful, upright person on the same level as the white majority, the lower-class African Americans demanded a push of black power and a certain degree of recompense. The most extreme form of this urge was illustrated in form of militant groups like the Black Panther movement. The urge to empower the black identity mostly among lower-class African Americans then partly resulted in the popularity of the Blaxploitation concept which functioned as a fictional compensation platform.

9

Guerrero elaborates the three main reasons for the emergence of Blaxploitation: Firstly, he states the rising political and social consciousness of African Americans partly in form of strong nationalistic impulses. Secondly, there must have been a big wave of critical dissatisfaction with Hollywood's degradation of blacks in film especially among black leaders, entertainers, and intellectuals, but also among the lower-class African-Americans. And thirdly, Hollywood was in a financial crisis in the late 1960s, which pushed the film industry to find a new economical source (69-71). Another condition enabling the realization of Blaxploitation was the loosening of obscenity laws by the Supreme Court, which led to a popular tolerance towards explicit sex, violence and graphic language in movies (Guerrero 94).

The first reason has been already introduced by the chapter before: The demand in the black audience for a black hero, who is ready to fight for his rights violently, rose and the implementation of the lower-class African American's resentment in these movies then satisfied many spectators with its aggressive display of black power. This urge and the demand of a change of the common degrading illustration of African Americans in film led to the boom of the Blaxploitation formula. The promise of financial success caused the film production company MGM to change the script of "Shaft" on short notice, which was originally written for a white protagonist and mostly white audience. Because of the high demand, they simply changed it to a black cast and context and it became one of the most successful Blaxploitation movies (Guerrero 91).

So, the Blaxploitation wave launched partly because of the African American protest but Guerrero sees the main reason in its profit: It was Hollywood's strategy to recover from its economic crisis (31). The film industry experienced a near economic collapse at the end of the 1960s because of the rise of television, a sudden change of attitudes among young filmgoers, and an increasing market of foreign films (82). The potential, which lay in the African American audience, had been a well-known fact in Hollywood since the mid-fifties though, as statistical estimations showed that black people made up 10 to 15 percent of the US-population at that time but about 30 percent of the audience in major-city theaters (Guerrero 83). So it is no surprise that the producers of Hollywood welcomed the financial potential they had found in this new form of cinematic exploitation.

Ironically, the same conditions that initially pushed the success of the genre also led to its end. While Hollywood appreciated the financial success of the films, it could explore new opportunities of film production and adapt to the then modern demand viewers, so that the film industry loosened its dependence on the exploitation and ceased it due to the surfeit of the genre (Guerrero 70). Additionally, Blaxploitation obviously did not match the requirements the black critics had not felt met already in beforehand. The depiction of blackness in the form of violence, poverty, drug-business, pimps, and gangsters was as degradingly using stereotypes as before. Jesse Jackson himself called on the black community to boycott Blaxploitation movies. Some of the main activist groups, including the National Association for the Advancement of Colored People (NAACP), the Congress of Racial Equality (CORE) and the Southern Christian Leadership Conference (SCLC), which all three criticized the genre's illustration of African Americanism since its emergence, formed the Coalition against Blaxploitation (CAB) in 1972. The CAB proposed a film rating system to openly display culturally pejorative works from their perspective (Guerrero 101).

4 The Portrayal of African Americanism in Blaxploitation

Besides the already mentioned features the protagonist hero is given in the Blaxploitation films, it is the aim of the following chapter to examine the general illustration of the African American identity in the genre. On that account, the Blaxploitation success Shaft will be analyzed and in this process also general characteristics of the genre's movies will be elaborated including a focus on the black female image created by them.

The reason I chose Shaft for the further analysis of the genre is rooted in the film's very appropriate representation of the genre's character. The film already has no entitlement to the genuineness of the starter SSBS, but answers the demands for the black powerful hero nevertheless by simply changing the film's script from a white context to a black. The mere arbitrariness with which the producers used the movie's content to be suited on demand represents the irrelevance of Blaxploitation movie's plots and their story's intentions. They only had to consist of a rough storyline functioning as disposable framework, which then could be filled and shaped repetitively with the same superficial formulaic content.

Costing only $1.2 million in production and leading to earnings of about $10.8 million after its first year of display, Shaft perfectly represents the success of the exploitation method (Guerrero 92). Its exploitative character made it a secure financial source and resulted in such disproportionate relations of financial input and output. Because of the supervision of MGM in the production, the movie came out less anti-white than SSBS, and therefore made it a bigger economic success attracting both black and white audiences. This also shows the superficiality of the illustration of black empowerment in many Blaxploitation movies. In the first line, the movies wanted to express the independence of African Americans from white Americans and the opportunities to enforce black interests, but in reality this aim could be cut back to compromise a greater financial benefit.

4.1.1 Background

Shaft was produced in 1971 and directed by the black filmmaker Gordon Parks under the supervision of the company MGM, which has been one of the most successful film studios of Hollywood until today. The soundtrack, including the title song which won the Oscar for the best song in film 1972, was composed by Isaac Hayes. The protagonist John Shaft is played by Richard Roundtree, who earned a disproportionate fee of $13,000 (Guerrero 92). Roundtree then had only appeared in one movie before: "What Do You Say to a Naked Lady?" in which he was in for one minute and had no line (James 18).

4.1.2 Plot

John Shaft is private detective in New York City, who is searched for by two police men in the beginning. One of the police men is Lieutenant Vic Androzzi. Shaft gets informed that some black gang members are looking for him and as he approaches his office, one of those men stands in the lobby of the building the office is situated in and waits for the protagonist. Shaft surprises him from behind and leads him to his office where another man is awaiting him already. After a short fight one of the men breaks through the window and falls to death. The other man tells Shaft that their mission was to bring him to their gang leader, the mobster Bumby. After that, Shaft is interrogated at the police station concerning the dead, who obviously fell out of his office's window. Shaft declares the incident an accident and holds back further information daring the high rank police man, who then unsatisfied leaves Shaft with Androzzi. By then it becomes noticeable that these two men have no hostile but a very tolerating if not amicable relationship.

Shaft then arranges a meeting with Bumpy in the office where the mobster explains that his daughter Marcy has been abducted and hires Shaft to return her. Shaft visits his girlfriend Ellie, who comforts him and has sex with him. For the purpose of Marcy's return Shaft should search for Ben Buford, who turns out to be a member of a black militant activist group. While meeting Buford, the group is attacked by unknown aggressors in a shooting and Shaft saves Buford, who then agrees to help him. After Shaft brings Buford to a save place at his friend's Dina, he meets with Vic, who explains that the shooting was aimed at Shaft and that a conflict between Bumpy's gang and the Italian mafia is upcoming. In reality, this conflict is only the problem between two gangs, but for the public perception it is a fight between black and white and he notices the possibility of a violent race war. When Shaft and Buford visit Bumpy, the mobster admits that his daughter has been captured by his Italian enemies and offers Shaft, Buford, and his militant comrades considerable amounts of money for the risky scheme to bring her pack.

Shaft then is informed that two members of the mafia are waiting for him to come home in a bar across the street. Shaft knows the gay bar keeper and asks him to mime the bartender to trick the two Italians and let them be arrested. After his successful scheme, Shaft invites the white woman Linda who had flirted with him in the bar, and they have sex in his apartment. Back in the police station, Shaft interrogates the two and receives information on a fellow Italian gang member, who can lead him to Marcy. Vic then admits to Shaft that this interrogation had been intercepted with a bugging device by the police and he has the order to take Shaft into custody, but lets him go to finish his mission officially using the excuse of not having him found. The protagonist uses the information received in the interrogation to find the place where Marcy is held captive and the situation results in a gun fight in which Shaft's shoulder is injured. After he got a medical treatment, he, Buford, and his men work out a plan to finally rescue Marcy. This plan is realized in a military like operation, in which the activists disguise as employees of the hotel, where the Italian mafia holds Marcy. After they have killed every present member of the mafia, Marcy is brought into a taxi provided by Bumpy, and Shaft calls Vic to inform him of his success.

4.2 Shaft! – Analysis

In the following analyses, I do not only want to present the contents in which the characteristics can be found that I am looking for, but I also intend to subsequently interpret those for a potential basis of evaluation in the end.

4.2.1 Plot Analysis

Shaft shows the usual characteristics of the aggressive and predominant black hero with a strong sexuality and masculinity. In contrast to other Blaxploitation films like SSBS, Shaft is able to cooperate with the white-dominated system in form of the police.

Although he counters the white men often in defiant and daring manner, he still is illustrated as an adapted detective – he seems contrarily but not revolutionary.

Guerrero interestingly presents evidence of Shaft's function as a symbolic middleman between black and white in the movie. Firstly, it is visible in his geographical situation. He lives in the Village, downtown New York City, his office is placed at the Time Square, midtown, and his primary place of investigation and interest is the uptown Harlem. The Village, being the New York center of artists and source of the 1960s counterculture, represents his hip and fashionable side. His workplace at the Time Square, which is the commercial and financial center of New York, shows his modern and business side giving him a connotation of typical white character. And his passion for Harlem finally shows the important bounds to the black community (92).

The second feature that Guerrero points out is the racial positioning of Shaft whereas he functions as mediator between black and white in form of the opposing criminal organizations (92). In my opinion, he does not really mediate between the two organizations, but rather show aversions towards both of them happening to work for the African Americans because of the financial reward and their threatening. Moreover, I would see him as a linkage between the white police and the black activists for both of whom he shows some kind of sympathy. In the end, he turns out to just use both of them for his own advantage when successfully ending his job.

The third feature of Guerrero is Shaft's sexual situation. On the one hand side he has a black girlfriend with whom the film even indicates he has some kind of intimate relationship apart from intercourse illustrated by their short conversations. On the other hand side Shaft sleeps around with a white woman and this behavior does not seem to be an exception. While it emphasizes his image of the sex machine, it also undermines his stance on the black side. Again, Guerrero argues for a mediating function of this aspect (93), whereas I think of it as an expression of an egoistic pursue of his own desire fulfillment.

In general, African Americans are mostly presented as dangerous or at least dubious in the movie. On the one hand side, we see a black, criminal organization similar to the Mafia, and there are also the violent and threatening black activists. Besides, there are loitering and 'shifty' blacks depicted in the streets, like the man Shaft asks for the place and time of the activist's meeting, who borrows the motif of the guy exchanging information for money. Naturally, there are also ordinary, black people like Shaft's girlfriend or the other people he questions while searching the activists, but these are noticeably in a minority. The film depicts white criminals, as well, but these fall into the common stereotype of 'Italian Mafia', which already is recognized as a form of 'white' more separated from the ordinary white, as it belongs to a certain nationality.

Although he seems rather adapted to his white surrounding, Shaft does not easily cooperate with the leaders of the police. His unwillingness to hand them over information on the window crash or the case of the abducted girl, and the fact that his interrogation of the Italian Mafiosi had been wire tapped, illustrates some kind of mutual distrust. For interpretation, this suspicion could be extended to a general distrust between the white leadership of federal institutions and African Americans who hold more power and possess more influence than the 'usual' lower-class black citizen. Moreover, one could argue we can see the assumption depicted there that the white, presumably conservative, leadership does not appreciate black success in the time of the Civil Rights Movement. Otherwise, the viewer could also interpret this distrust as the unwillingness of the police to let important work done by an allegedly amateur.

The only male character that could be described as some kind of friend to Shaft is Lt. Vic Androzzi, apart from Shaft's black female friends Ellie and Dina. Androzzi and Shaft share information, fun, and a certain degree of mutual trust. The climax of their relationship in the movie is represented in the scene, in which Androzzi refuses to arrest Shaft and lets him finish his mission. Their relationship can be seen as a symbol for the chance of black and white friendship.

The fact that the conflict between the rivaled criminal organizations could probably be perceived as a race war is a reason for interpretation of a possible criticism of the general black and white thinking in public. Instead of questioning the background of violent conflicts, the majority simply constitutes their roots in racial tensions.

In the end, one can see the winners and losers of the movie rather clearly. The white criminals obviously lost the battle, as all of them who appeared in the story had been killed, and their plan of extortion by abduction failed with the rescue of Marcy. This fact presumably shows that crime in general cannot win. The African American criminal organization on the other hand achieved its goal to outplay the Italian scheme and regain the leader's daughter, but as the organization was not powerful enough to do it itself Bumpy and his men seem rather harmless or at least less threatening than before. Black crime then gets off lightly while it neither really experiences negative consequences, nor has it to fear legal prosecution by federal institutions. Meanwhile, the police could not yet enforce its authority concerning the criminal organizations or Shaft himself, so they are perceived as rather impotent. The black activists join the operation ultimately for money to have some of their members released from prison, which indicates that they care for each other. They could prove their skills in the rescue operation, although they possibly would not have been successful without the help of Shaft. So the audience could receive the image of the activists as skillful fighters, who help criminals, but nevertheless fight for African American interests even if they are just their own.

Eventually, John Shaft is the clear winner of the plot. He successfully rescued Marcy, hence accomplished his mission, until then avoided legal prosecution by the police, and the viewer gets the impression that nothing would have succeeded without him. So from the plot, one could either argue that the African American characters in general were the winners of the story, as every one of them achieved their goals and performed well. On the other hand side though, Shaft could be seen as the only real winner, because the others still had to experience negative side effects, like loss of authority and reputation for Bumby and his men, as well as casualties on the side of the activists. Only Shaft suffers no harm besides his shot wound, which shows that he too is human but does not stop him anyway. So the fact that Shaft is the only real winner of the movie indicates that not African Americanism is celebrated here, but solely the individual hero of the film, which again illustrates his substitutionality.

4.2.2 Film Analysis

Right in the introduction sequence of the movie, when Shaft walks along the streets, we can see a black man offering him a watch on the sidewalk. The intended transaction is implicitly illegal and illustrates criminal street activity carried out by African American. Shaft wears a leather jacket, cloth trousers and a turtleneck pullover all in beige or brown colors. James states that these earth tone colors should associate with the African origin of blacks in the USA and were a prevalent symbol for African Americanism at the time of the Civil Rights Movement (James 14). Afterwards Shaft uses the service of a black shoe polisher, which indicates a common field of African American profession. The protagonist seems to know members of the lower urban daily life well, which can also be observed when talking to the white blind news stand owner. The film depicts that Shaft, as a representation of black men, knows the urban life and its members and they stand in a familiar relationship. The common mutual appellation of African Americans in the film is "brother" or "baby", as Shaft demonstrates firstly in the shoe shine shop by saying:

17

"Thanks brother.", or as he leaves: "We're straight baby." (Shaft). The appellation of baby then also applies for white people expressing seemingly a very casual social interaction from the perspective of Shaft giving him a 'cool' attitude, as it can be seen in scene, where Androzzi warns him of the dangers of his job at the police station. In addition, this nonchalance of Shaft seems to enable him to maintain a rather disrespectful manner of communication with especially white people. Examples for that can be observed in the first contact of him and Androzzi and his colleague or him talking to the high rank police man at the police station. In that very scene, Androzzi also asks him why the two African Americans from Shaft's office carried so many weapons and Shaft replies that it is a common procedure among blacks to not "go around" without means of self-defense anymore (Shaft). This could be interpreted as a resemblance to the African American vigilance and willingness to fight back when being threatened in the time of the Civil Rights Movement. Also Shaft states that he would never beg for help from the police, which presumably represents a certain black pride and the will of African American to be independent from the institutional establishment, which is implicitly led by white men. On the other hand side, Androzzi replies to Shaft, what this "black shit" was which African Americans argued with permanently. He possibly alludes to the criticism on the perceived habit of African Americans to find the reasons of conflict between them and white people in racial tension. As Shaft leaves, a taxi attempting to stop for him drives on, as the driver notices a white man calling a taxi and ignores Shaft consequently; this shows an act of white preference.

Shaft then talks to Bumby and later explains in his grief for his daughter that she is expected to go to college. The audience can interpret this statement as a wish for African Americans to experience the same opportunities as white people by attending high educational institutions and in prospect achieve prestigious positions. In the following montage, which is musically accompanied by a song by Hayes about the struggle of black people for equality and against the poor conditions in black inner-city communities, Shaft is shown talking to various black and white people to gather information. In the montage we can see again that Shaft has a direct and trustful connection to the lower-class citizens of New York City. By financially helping out a shivering boy at the stairs of an apartment building, the film certainly illustrates the mutual care among African Americans in the ghetto. What follows, is the sequence in which Shaft meets the black activist group. He outplays the door guards by simply using the back door, so the first impression of the activists presents them as rather naïve and badly organized. The members of the group recognize Shaft from the "old days"; presumably they met before at events of African American protest against inequality. In the background, there is a poster of Malcom X, who represents a more radical form of Civil Rights' protest. The scene possesses a hostile mood, as the activists see Shaft as conform to the system and accuse him of having betrayed the African American interests. Furthermore, he is confronted with accusations of working for the white men and thinking like one of them, after he flew from the gun fight with Buford. The activists are depicted as big mouthed in their accusations, but they cannot back up their provoking attitude as Shaft talks back to them. He seems definitely more intelligent and sovereign than them and consequently superior. This impression fortifies when Shaft's friend Dina rebukes Buford for his loud and rude tone in her apartment and he responds childishly by looking to the ground with an ashamed face.

In the scene that Shaft calls his girlfriend in she asks him if he got problems. Shaft replies with: "Yeah, I got a lot of them. I was born black and I was born poor." (Shaft). Here the protagonist supposes an inevitable connection of being a poor African American and having trouble leading a decent life. It seems as if such people are condemned to a lack of prospects and a legally and financially unworried existence.

Having slept with the white woman from the bar, Shaft requests her to go as he is busy. She is offended by his discourteous behavior and as he asks her to close the after leaving, she replies with "Close it yourself, shitty!" (Shaft). Obviously, Shaft has no problems using a woman for sex and ignoring her afterwards to mind his business.

Lastly, there is the sequence of the rescue operation that is carried out by the activists in a very militant, commando-like manner. The men wear commando hats and berets and are dressed in a uniformed black, before they disguise as hotel personnel. In combat with the Italian gangsters, the activists skillfully strike their opponents with accurate hits, sometimes using the common action film motif of striking a man intentionally unconscious with one punch in the neck. The operation proceeds not without a wounded activist, who is not left behind in the gun fight. So eventually, the black activists are depicted as skillful combaters, who are not intellectually but violently dangerous in respect to the first meeting of Shaft and them.

In the last scene, Shaft casually walks out the hotel and into a telephone booth to call Androzzi and hand him over the "case". After Androzzi asks him to close the case, he only replies with: "Close it yourself, shitty.", and walks away laughing.

Guerrero describes the role of women in the Blaxploitation starter SSBS as only existent through the male-female relationship of men needing help or comfort, or simply using women as prostitutes (91). Van Peebles even admitted that including attractive women principally served the purpose of a higher economic value by the formula "sex sells" (91). In most Blaxploitation movies women were awarded no political stand and most often they functioned as the sexual objectification for the male hero.

In Shaft there is some ambiguity concerning the portrayal of women. Shaft's girlfriend is introduced before the first sex scene by entering her apartment carrying grocery bags which she immediately drops at the kitchen counter to comfort Shaft, who already waits for her on the couch half-naked. Here we can interpret her as symbol for the housewife responsible for the housework and the well-being of her man. After Shaft stayed overnight at hers and communicated his worries with her, whereby she only approves of his statements, he leaves to return to his work. Thus, Ellie seems as a means to relief himself of his sorrow. Dina, on the other hand side, proves to be an upright and proud black woman, who does not condone discourtesy at her home and is not afraid to articulate her interests, as it is shown in the scene after Shaft rescued Buford from the gun assault. This could also be a result of her being a mother to two children, having learned to cope with such form of impoliteness. Bumpy's daughter Marcy borrows the motif of the woman in need, that has to be saved from the villains, and the red-haired Linda from the bar enjoys intercourse with Shaft, but is not afraid to pronounce her opinion on Shaft's behavior. So the film shows both a powerful and proud, but also needy and weak image of women.

Popular examples of powerful women in Blaxploitation are presented by the movies "Cleopatra Jones" (1973), played by Tamara Jones, and "Foxy Brown" (1974), played by Pam Grier, who starred as an homage to the original character in the Quentin Tarantino film "Jackie Brown" in 1997. These two characters demonstrated that also black women knew how to fight and shoot and outplay their enemy men with their intelligence. Ross states that they appeared strong, independent and threatening to majority figures like whites, men or the establishment, but finally they remained feminine and vulnerable (19). There foremost purpose, though, was their attractive and sexy appealing to the male audience. To do so as well for the white, male viewers, these women fulfilled sexual preferences according to the common white male: They had an athletic body and often wore long, straight hair instead of the more preferred Afro hairdo among blacks. Reid suggests that they served an urge in the white, male audience's imagination to oppress these women's sexual and racial power (qtd. in Ross 19). In addition, Ross claims that their violence most often was directed against other women, which eliminated the potential threat of female solidarity for males. Contrary to that, Foxy Brown castrates the male villain at the end of the movie and sends his testicles to his woman (Guerrero 99). The symbol of this action is obviously a sign of female superiority, but still not of female solidarity. In the end however, the black heroine is said to return into the accommodation of her "lover" (19).

5 Evaluation of the Impact of Blaxploitation on the Image of African Americans

5.1 Black Film – Before, Then, Afterwards

At least, the cinematic image of African Americans changed from powerless and quiet to boisterous and sovereign due to the illustrations of Blaxploitation. It apparently gave the black audience a feeling of insurgency against the superficial appeasement strategy of black presentation the years before. Melvin Van Peebles stated that black film work became meaningful when it attracted a wide audience – therefore it had to abandon didactic tendencies (Ross 63). This dominance of entertainment towards information and education is due to the fact that greater movie productions were expensive at the time of Blaxploitation and still are. It adds that filmgoers wanted to be entertained and one could not as easily attract people to watch an informative film as pure entertainment (Ross 63). Meanwhile, a contrary form of film came out depicting a more or less open suppression of African Americans due to their perceived criminal majority. An example of the fight against black revolt in this sense is the movie "Dirty Harry" (1971) starring Clint Eastwood. This development shows that the Blaxploitation euphoria also had its counterpart, whereas it remains speculative whether or not Blaxploitation triggered it. Nevertheless, the genre prepared way for all-black film productions and a wave of black actors in demand. After 1975, the tendency emerged that black producers created more authentic and serious illustrations of the regular and ordinary life, including the necessary bitterness and pessimism to show poverty and the lack of prospects in black, inner-city life. The motif of the race clash and the black and white confrontation declined in the 1980s and black filmmakers noticed that also not exclusively black-focused movies could appeal to the African American audience. Also the fact that white viewers would watch works with a focus on black content lowered the aggression of those movies (Guerrero 105). Criticism on inequality and racism became more serious and a wave of black comedy started in the 1980s, as well. Only in the late 1980s and early 1990s black film reached a new high in terms of violence. Then the emerging Hip-Hop culture and the urban "'Hood life" provoked the cinematic transfer of this then modern gang culture (Ross 71).

Finally, the question is to be answered if Blaxploitation served as a mean for African American empowerment, or was it only a more subtle and masked form of black devaluation in film? Ross argues that, besides introducing a new set of stereotypes and being more provocative than informative, SSBS and Superfly can be considered examples of a thoughtful transfer of black interests and social criticism in films. They especially illustrated the unfair and inevitable inability of African Americans in the ghettoes to live to the standard of the ordinary white person and, furthermore, the white man's guilt in the denial of possible opportunities for them (63). Riley mentioned that the genre was nothing more than an imitation of the traditional action movie reproduced with a black cast. It was an expression of pure unreality in black life in order to reassure white expectations of African Americans and repress their political consciousness (qtd. in Guerrero 93). By that, he means that the black spectators knew that the hero and his success for blackness they were seeking did not apply to reality. While most of them condemned the violence, the negative illustration of the black community and the massive depiction of black crime, they nevertheless celebrated the black hero, standing straight for their ideals. Of course, they were conscious of the implausibility of that and the knowledge to be confronted with the every-day racism in reality again. This romanticizing of ghetto life in contrast to the grim reality had been an opportunity to leave the latter for about one-and-a-half hours.

The ambiguous portrayal of the black activists lay in their representation of a hope for black empowerment and their depiction as strong institution, but on the other hand side their illustration between the lines was naïve, unsuccessful and without prospect on a conceivable improvement of their fight for black power. Related to this, Shaft asked Buford after he saved him why they (the activists) are standing still when running a revolution (Shaft). Black Panther activist Huey Newton condemned Blaxploitation films as counter-revolutionary singling out SSBS. They presented the black threat on the white system as naïve and unlikely (qtd. in Ross 19, 20). Tony Brown assessed the genre as "symptomatic for black self-hate" and dangerous in its glorification of crime and violence, as well as the high potential of uncritical identification of viewers with the 'heroes' (qtd. in Ross 20). These heroes were static figures, showed no development, and acted selfishly to reach their individualistic goals - an argument that also coincides with my analysis and interpretation of Shaft's procedure.

What possibly appeals to many viewers in contrast to the desexualized African American film image before is the then potent, desirable hero, who is sexually skilled and experienced. In terms of black identity, this aspect could also serve to distance oneself from the white, American masculinity, which in film exceeded the black masculinity, but was perceived less superior in reality in terms of sexual desirability and performance. Critics however disapproved of the picture drawn in the genre and stated that black manhood did not equal high skill and frequency of intercourse, and that women would not only serve to satisfy these needs (Guerrero 90).

Nevertheless, Guerrero says these pictures, that were drawn by the films, not only concerning the sexual exploitation, were images of something that existed at that time even if it did not match the anticipated skills some African American intellectuals wanted to achieve (90). The genre's real life influence had some noticeable dimension: Being called 'Sweetback', referring to SSBS, applied for very sexually active men in every-day, inner-city black language. Further effects of the films SSBS and Superfly on its audience were, for example, a new hype of leather jackets, pimp clothes, chemically straightened locks instead of the Afro hairdo, and a wave of successful movie merchandise. Superfly also resulted in a hype of wide sideburns along with straight hair among blacks and an increase of customized Cadillacs on the streets of ghetto communities. The most significant side effect of this film, though, was an increase of cocaine consumption among inner-city, black youths (Guerrero 96, 97). Again, one could argue that the films only portrayed real life conditions in the ghettoes and that these conditions therefore intensified by themselves.

In the end, it is obvious that the Blaxploitation movies polarized and some structures crystallize in their perception. The criticism on the genre mostly emanated from the higher-class, intellectual African Americans, whereas lower-class colored Americans welcomed the films at least in the beginning and found compensation for their resentments. Finally, the question persists on how to evaluate the image this genre created about African Americans and their life.

6 Conclusion

Previously, this paper examined the causes and backgrounds of Blaxploitation, gave a lot of examples and pictures of the characterization of African Americanism in the genre, and explained some arguments for the critical perception of these films.

The most essential characteristics illustrated showed a powerful, aggressive, potent, and sexually active and skilled black man, who is able to fight the mostly white superiority and cares for his black community. African Americans among themselves are usually depicted in a process of mutual help, but also in mutual distrust. The black, militant activism often is portrayed as naïve and as condemned to be unsuccessful, which could be interpreted as appearing discouraging for enthusiasts of such activity, but frankly, I think no activist in the 1970s USA reality would let himself demoralize by some B-movies.

Certainly, the genre of Blaxploitation generated and strengthened some stereotypical images of African Americanism especially in a subcultural way. The figure of the pimp wearing a fur coat, shiny necklaces and carrying an extravagant cane remains popular until today's illustration in the hip-hop culture. The black cop working for racial justice in collaboration with his or her white partner developed from Shaft to Miami Vice and Lethal Weapon. Doubtless, Blaxploitation also helped African American men to a certain reputation of advanced sexual performance skills and a high libido. So some characteristics presented in these films of the 1970s have been present and developed in aspects of African American cultural representation unto this day.

The illustration of women in these films has to be estimated as mainly negative. They served as sexual objectification for both black and white male viewers, even when they played the main role. I think it was more the attitude of the time than of the genre itself to give women that little authenticity. Also, it lies not within the intention of the nature of action films until this very day to give an authentic depiction of anything other than violence and the means to carry it out. In general, I think it is true to say that Blaxploitation as well lacked authenticity in almost every aspect. That is why filmmakers afterwards intensified in this intention as explained before.

The black community has been depicted in a more romanticized way as it really appeared. Of course, that created a new stereotype of black environment including drugs, prostitution, and crime, and euphemized the conditions in such areas, but I am certain that most viewers were conscious of this contrast and did not interchange media with reality. I do not want to ignore the real negative side effects that could have influenced the audience in form of an increase of drug consumption in inner-city communities and a questionable form of identification for especially young viewers, including the use of violence and disrespect towards women. However, the dispute on the effects of media on young people, notably in terms of violence and sexuality, has an old tradition and never really proved that these illustrations would influence people to imitate them.

Finally, you cannot answer the question whether Blaxploitation had a positive or a negative impact on the image of black people. It was full of unauthentic stereotypes of the inner-city African American life, which, on the other hand side, only illustrated real life conditions. Curtis Mayfield said accordingly, that the depiction of social reality showing drug-pushing and consumption, black crime, and other downsides of the ghetto life would be continuing as long as those conditions existed. If people were dissatisfied with the movies they should eliminate those conditions instead of the films (qtd. in Guerrero 102). Of course, criticism is always justified when supported by good arguments and the criticism on Blaxploitation was – in my opinion, but I also think that these films did not harm the image of African Americans nor did it effectively harm the audience in general. I do not want to deny that their illustration also caused people to behavior one would principally assess as negative, but all films have the potential to do so.

The stereotypical depiction of African Americanism, on the other side, presumably did not help the present endeavors to establish a general idea of a differentiated image of black people in the late 1960s and early 1970s. However, I think the problem behind that lies not in the films itself but in the people, who transfer such stereotypical images to every African American. To help such people, one would have to change the conditions causing this way of thinking in the first place.

As always, it is the task and privilege of every individual recipient to decide for him or herself whether to review the Blaxploitation films' portrayal and impact as positive or negative. For myself, I am of the opinion that this genre did not influence the general perception of African Americanism in a way it would have harmed the struggle for racial equality. It may have influenced some people negatively, idolizing the films or obtaining their African American image solely from this genre, but in the long sight it has been entertaining people, and perhaps gave some a feeling of hope and pride to overcome the negative conditions shown in the genre, as well as to celebrate the excessive pictures it delivered.

7 Bibliography

Diawara, Manthia. *Black American Cinema.* New York; London: Routledge, 1993.

Guerrero, Ed. *Framing Blackness. The African American Image in Film.* Philadelphia: Temple University Press, 1993.

James, Darius. *That's Blaxploitation! Roots of the Baadasssss 'Tude.* New York: St. Martin's Griffin, 1995.

Ross, Karen. *Black and White Media. Black Images in Popular Film and Television.* Cambridge: Polity Press, 1996.

Shaft. Dir. Gordon Parks. Perf. Richard Roundtree. MGM, 1971. Film

YOUR KNOWLEDGE HAS VALUE

- We will publish your bachelor's and
  master's thesis, essays and papers

- Your own eBook and book -
  sold worldwide in all relevant shops

- Earn money with each sale

Upload your text at www.GRIN.com
and publish for free

CPSIA information can be obtained
at www.ICGtesting.com
Printed in the USA
LVHW091321060220
645827LV00013B/1432

9 783668 740587